CONNIE B

Central
Reservations

NEW & SELECTED POEMS

BLOODAXE BOOKS

ISBN: 1 85224 128 4

First published 1990 by
Bloodaxe Books Ltd,
P.O. Box 1SN,
Newcastle upon Tyne NE99 1SN.

Bloodaxe Books Ltd acknowledges
the financial assistance of Northern Arts.

Typesetting by Bryan Williamson, Darwen, Lancashire.

Printed in Great Britain by
Bell & Bain Limited, Glasgow, Scotland.

*For Felicity, Chris,
John, Steve, Jill*

Acknowledgements

The poems in the first two sections are selected from Connie Bensley's collections *Progress Report* (1981) and *Moving In* (1984), both published by Peterloo Poets.

For poems in the third section, acknowledgements are due to the editors of the following publications in which some of those poems first appeared: *Cosmopolitan, The Faber Book of Fevers and Frets*, edited by D.J. Enright (1989), *Illuminations, The Literary Review, New Statesman, The Observer, P.E.N. New Poetry II* (Quartet Books, 1988), *The Poetry Book Society Anthology 1989-1990* (PBS/Hutchinson, 1989), *Poetry Review, Prospice, Psychopoetica, Slipping Glimpses* (Poetry Book Society Supplement, 1985), *The Spectator, Times Literary Supplement, Vision On*, and *With a Poet's Eye* (Tate Gallery, 1986).

'Heaven on Earth' and 'Two Pheasants' were broadcast on *Poetry Now* (BBC Radio 3). 'A Friendship' won first prize in the 1986 Cheltenham Festival Poetry Competition, 'Puzzle Picture' won 3rd prize in the 1988 Leek International Poetry Competition, and 'The Badminton Game' won 2nd prize in the Tate Gallery competition in 1986.

Contents

CENTRAL RESERVATIONS

Daily Round

The Stronger Sex

Seeing Things

Attachments

FROM **PROGRESS REPORT**

(1981)

Annual Dinner

I have sat here at this table now for years.
I have a race memory of this place;
Its formal flora, face-distorting spoons,
And the indigenous tribes, of bearers and borers.

Sometimes I dance, held hot against black serge,
And often I ask,
Shouting above the music,
About Croydon, or the Common Market, or the children.

Before the dancing we had the speeches,
And that was a peaceful time.
An interval of pleasant stupefaction
Infused with coffee and brandy.

Further back still, there was the cream gâteau
And, penetrating deeper layers of the past,
The lamb, the trout, the soup,
And, with each, a subject briskly explored,
To right and to left,
With eye contact and ego projection.

In the prehistoric, previous world
I was still here,
Empty and chattering over gin,
And smiling winningly into unfamiliar faces.

But, unlike some younger people,
I can still remember the world outside,
And I know that one day we will all go home
And find rest, and the cat waiting to be fed.

April

Here comes Spring.
Season (stirring dull blood) of spots
And suicides.
Better, those of us who are at risk
To skip April, May,
Miss the worst of the disorientation,
The conviction that life
Is coming up with some colossal romantic musical
For which the casting director has, yet again,
Overlooked you.

The hard light, the sudden knife-like breeze,
The grey pallor of those strips of skin
So tentatively bared.
The tender vulnerability of the pale buds in the hedge.

Dig up the garden
And stop your mind with your transistor.
This dangerous change will soon pass.

Cardiac Department

Discrete, disconsolate,
The heart patients gather in the waiting-room.
Drawn together, but facing apart
And thinking about their ECGs.

They'd like to pretend
They're in the buffet at King's Cross
Waiting for the 6.15:
But more serious matters are at stake:
Life insurance; or life itself.

The nurse is their mother here,
Her smiles flow out
Bright and inexhaustible as conjurors' bunting.

The cleaner is having a mysterious mid-morning clean.
'Don't move love,' she says,
'Don't move. I can dust round you.'

Comfort

In a meadow, redolent of summer,
Deep in green, each leaf gilded
Against the sky, sit three women
Smiling at the camera. They are fat
Beyond the merely Rubenesque.

Corseted in folding chairs,
Armoured in synthetics;
Their considerable legs stretch forward in unison.
In the East, they would be collectors' pieces.

One has a striped umbrella
Over her head. She suffers with the sun.
Another has the thermos, which she's handing on to Flo,
For Flo gets parched; and all of them are kind.

Indeed, if you were lost – if you had missed the path
That led back round the hill
They'd help you; they would hem you in
And wall you round with helpfulness.

Such a stockade:
No harm could penetrate.
You'd be safe there,
Safe, and in clover.

Commuter

Coke tins glisten in the showery gutters,
The turd-strewn grass is springing rank and green.
Dull glass catches light it had forgotten
And I am expected home on the six-fifteen.

In the warmth, my briefcase is relaxing;
The non-press collar manacles my neck.
Steam is rising from my pinstripe suiting.
I feel the message, but can I answer back?

My hand on the telephone is winter white.
It clams to the plastic. No one answers my call.
What can I do but order stones and piping,
Get to my garden, build a waterfall?

Crossing London to Suffolk

After the roadworks,
After the plastic shops and dusty gutters,
The tombstone flats rooted in concrete.

After the scrawled walls,
The town-grey faces,
The hard-edge brick and metalwork

Comes the first field:
Gold – tiger-striped
Where the stubble has been burned,

Blue pulled right down behind it:
Set and enmeshed
In cool green places,

Dreamed up by the inward urban eye
For summer. Yet in winter,
Under pewter light,

The neon shops and claustrophobic streets
Will pull me back to warmth and ugliness;
Home again, like a cat to the cupboard it knows.

Desires

Newly shaven, your eyes only slightly bloodshot,
Your rat-trap mouth smiling up at the corners,
You remind me of the Head Girl
I used to be in love with.

It's something about your sporty build,
The way you seem to be counting the people in the café
With a view to lining them up in teams.

It's quite set me in the mood for the evening,
And I follow you alertly through the door,
Hoping you'll turn and snap at me
To pick my feet up, and not to slouch.

Dig

Music, raucous behind the bushes,
Drew me into the graveyard.

A man was digging for the next incumbent,
Down to his elbows, his trannie by his side.

Man and bird, and Presley,
Raised their voices to heaven.

'You need a bit of a song,' said the man,
'When you're working to a deadline.'

Dropping Out

I planned to write this thesis, you see,
On cooking and personality –

You know the sort of thing:
The exhibitionist who flambés at table,
The introvert, who hides his food in pastry,
The impulsive griller,
The contemplative casseroler,
And the rigid, repressed personality
Who has to have each ingredient
Down to the last grain.

Unfortunately I overdid the practical work:
Became immersed in my theories,
Testing, tasting – wasting my spirit
In a lust for pasta,
Becoming, at last, a compulsive eater.

'You're trying to fill a void,' they said,
And sent me up to the Tavistock.

But somehow my problems made the analyst hungry.
We took to cooking ourselves bijou meals
And lying down to discuss them,
Whiling away whole nights
In psychogastric speculation.

That man has really taught me a thing or two,
And his light touch with a soufflé
Has quite made me forget my academic career.

The Emigré

What land is that, stained out
Across the wall?
I think I knew it when I was a boy.

Twisting my neck on the pillow
I can see the coast,
And that inlet – the grey shading into the shallows –
Where the village was.

My mother wore blue serge
Down to her boots.
The yard had a sunflower, so high
It looked in at my window.

There is the river where I used to fish
And never thought of time.

Here, all our time's paid out in tiny sips
And clocked by pills, and wiped away with gauze.

Yesterday they propped me up in bed.
Tomorrow I may get across the room
And see it all, once more.

Evidence

*'It is alleged that the incident took place
during a holiday in France.'*

Did intimacy take place?
Difficult to be sure.

Hands whispered over sunwarmed skin.
Murmurs, through tangled hair,
Were fervid. There was, perhaps –
Can one recall –
Some interpenetration of the flesh
In the shafting half-light from the afternoon blinds.

Movements and time were mindless;
Half-entranced by the clock's tick
And the clip of the blown vines
On the trellis wall.

But was there a world outside?
Or was it a room that was traced in the sand
(Where the incoming tide lapped a regular pulse)
By the hand of the dreamer, who seemed in his sleep
To feel salt lips on his closed eyes
In the dim room, with the clock's tick
And the tap of the vines in the faint breeze
From the warm sea
As it sighed, outside.

Father Christmas

Last year's Father Christmas
Caught pneumonia and died
Through standing in the shopping precinct
Shaking his tin in all weathers
Under the municipal Christmas tree.

This year's Father Christmas is of wax,
Sitting on a stool, apple cheeked
And smiling without relief,
His tin intimately lodged between his knees.

He watches the lights change
(Green to amber, amber to red)
With bland accord.
It is the nature of things.

Yesterday someone fell under wheels
Before his very eyes,
Crying out, and bleeding in a Christmassy colour;
And he smiled and smiled,
Never turning his head at the ambulance bell
Or envying the attentions of the crowd.

February

February, a poor month for the foot fetishist:
Wellingtons, old clodhoppers,
Socks that have almost breathed their last,
And when the occasional foot is glimpsed, naked,
By the determined voyeur,
It is deathly pale and flabby,
Contoured and moulded by the winter boot,

And, though fascinating, hardly contemporary:
More like something unearthed from a previous season.

But dream hotly, you fellow fetishists
Of a spell in March,
When the weather may break, and evoke
The first disturbing sandals of the year.

Genes

Someone asked me: 'Why are you smiling?'

I was remembering my father:
Pottering in the garden,
Mild, white haired, ironical,
Always waiting for the nine o'clock news,
Always going in for competitions and unusual diets.

In the First War he came upon a German soldier
And they surrendered to each other simultaneously.

Which reminds me from whom I must have learned
Always to take the line of least resistance.

God's Christmas Jokes

Christmas: there was the usual crop of disasters:
Planes, coaches, crashed.
(So often the victims are pilgrims
Or those on errands of mercy).

In the home, the disasters are on a less heroic scale,
The stressful, claustrophobic press
Of one's nearest and dearest
Being by far the worst.

The snappy rejoinders, early on suppressed,
And by Day Three not suppressed.
The bathroom used for a quick fit of sobbing
And phone calls late at night
From suicidal single friends
Who have missed out on Perfect Love at Christmas.

On the first day after Bank Holiday the Sales begin,
And people shoot out from their doors like prisoners released,
Glad to be finished with their attempts at Peace on Earth
And bursting with meaty energy for the fray.

Hiatus

Ragworn with our emotions, out of sight
Of reason; ash-trays brimming by the bed,
We drag on through the fitful, racked-out night
Reiterating all that we have said
Ten times or more before, and still it fails
To lead us from the maze.
                                        At last the dawn
Prefigures some release. The window pales.
I rest my head against it. On the lawn
I see the starlings quarrel, strut and jerk,
(Like some old newsreel, grainy black and grey),
Their energies close-channelled to their work:
Survival. Well they manage, so we may:
The day will come, and like awaited rain,
Will make our lives move forward once again.

In the Hospital Gardens

I kick the bush and it spouts silver.
All that dew, all those roses,
All that intricate coloured stuff
Is making me see red.

So impersonal, this leafwork,
No voice, no hand, no help.
Only beauty, and shining crystal drops
Staring bloody back at me.

Perhaps if I stay
Forcing back the gall,
Trying to be calm,
Something may stir and lift its head.

24

But I know my need is more than vegetable.
Those flat leaves cannot help me,
Or those thin cold stalks
Threading up from the bone-yards.

Kiss

As she left, she kissed him.
The touch fused amazing messages to his mind,
Upsetting fine checks and balances,
Invading and nourishing closed parts.

Layers melted from his skin.
On the instant, his life regressed
To mouth and hands. To clinging
In case of getting lost.

She drew away from him.
As he turned, he seemed to be himself,
But in his head he bayed, like the dog
When he kept it, chained, outside.

Life Study

Dawn or dusk may find me,
Pressed well back into the landscape,
Crumbs in hand.

The stealth, the immobility, the bone-aching patience
Come easily to me.

So what chance do you have?
I have marked you down.
No force is necessary, except in my mind;
And slowly, by my graduated rewards,
You will come to my hand.

March

That night, the wind caught in the drainpipe,
Howling in tongues,
Frightening him upright in the bed.

The garbled message sent his heart wild to help –
Squeezing, jetting, damming,
Gushing, syncopating, fibrillating,
And finally cancelling itself out.

'How nice for him' they said, at daybreak,
'To slip away quietly in his sleep.'

May

They're cutting grass below in Lincoln's Inn,
And by her desk, soft air is drifting in
With hints of lilac. Seven hours to go
Between these walls. 'Dear Sir,' the hours begin.

'Dear Sir,...My dearest Sir' her fingers say
(With carbon copies) 'write to me today,
And tell me what you look like, who you are,
And if you feel the summer on its way.'

Nature Study

It was a bad scene,
This badger in the graveyard,
Archaeologist-keen, industrious to a fault.

In the early dawn
He burrowed under MAUD JEFFERSON,
SPINSTER OF THIS PARISH,
Elbowing her headstone awry.

Hardly stopping to nibble the bulb roots
He grunted and delved: what he dug up
Looked suspiciously lumpy in the half light.

Pawing through light and shade, stone and earth,
His family gathered round,
Hungry and curious, shuffling the rubble,
Sensing, perhaps, that it was picnic time.

1915

Those mothers: how could they bear it?
Did they tear up the yellowing snapshots:

That picnic when he fell into the pond;
The outing with the Sunday school
(Scowling, mutinous, in the second row);
The cricket match; more groups, and last of all,
His first leave.
                        He's almost finished, here,
With childish things.

Fresh-faced, wide-eyed he turns. He's on his way
To the muddy abattoir.

Lucky for us, whose children survive to mortgages
And greyness.

Parent and Child

See the parent and the child
Tossed by tides.

We try to tread rational waters,
But something darker closes over our heads,
Sweeping us apart and dashing us together.

Words cannot explain: they fuse with the wind,
Leaving the faces naked, the arms waving.

Sometimes a body is beached, gasping.

Turn it over with your foot.
One side is white, the other side is black.

Paterfamilias

The house is uneasy with adolescents.
One is on the phone, under a tent of hair,
One is making tea again,
And several, in strangling jeans,
Are letting each other
In and out of the front door.

Well it's nothing to do with me,
As we'd all be the first to admit.

But somehow the ambience, cool and discordant, like the music,
Seeps under the door
And between me and the printed page.

Is there an atavistic element in my disquiet?
Some ancient ousting from a headship of the tribe,
Or herd?

I think it is just the feeling that they are not *tamped down*:
That the veneer may not hold.

Permissive Society

Wake, for the dawn has put the stars to flight,
   And in my bed a stranger: so once more,
What seemed to be a good idea last night
   Appears, this morning, sober, rather poor.

Post Mortem

Here are the body contents.
Bundling them out, like washing from a sink,
Is somehow too cursory;
Lacking both in greed and reverence.

The figure lies back, plundered,
Blueing and greening where the skin holds.
The colours are too bold for this ice palace,
They rate a hot, vulture-wheeling plain.

But the knives are out now, slicing into the tissues,
Bringing them, lovely as wallpaper, to the microscopes,
And giving things away – the woodbines, the pints,
The chips, the indolence.

It is the new telling of the entrails,
The new intimacy.
Too late to hang the *Do Not Disturb* sign
Over his doorknob.

Progress Report

Programming, in middle age, goes badly wrong:
Inside, the personality,
Richer (with luck), more rewarding,
Feeling a mature 21 at last:

But outside, one incredulously sees
The flesh convexing and relaxing;
The skin, like an ageing suitcase,
Recording much exposure and a few knocks;
The pigment perversely leaving the hair
And turning up in blotches on the face.

But the hormones still ebb and flow
With tiresome incongruity.
Wrong again, God.
You should have given us glands with built-in obsolescence,
Or better quality bodywork.

Provence

Provence, a name like perfumed air,
Warm fruit, herbs fragrant underfoot,
Emerald lizards,
And the sun, the sun,
Hot but not punishing:
Enough to dry the silver swimmer's skin
Before he pours the wine into his glass.

The small hotel, though vaguely picturesque,
Was dark, and had a queasy smell inside.
It wasn't quite as in the Michelin Guide.
The beds weren't made. Nobody at the desk.

Along the river banks the dream comes right,
But first you have to park your baking car.
They charge a lot. The heat dissolves the tar.
But then you see the swallowtails in flight
And if you walk on in the sweating sun,
The other, dreamed Provence, will have begun.

Recluse

This house is becoming inappropriate.
I am shrinking out of it:
Rattle about like a pea in a casket.

It used to fit me:
Now my voice echoes thinly in the corridors,
And lamplight fades out
Before it reaches the cold walls.

It used to be an ordinary size:
Now I sit uneasily in its cavern mouth,
Crouch in cupboards,
Move only with my back to the skirting-board.

Once somebody knocked,
But even in those days I could not reach the keyhole
To see who was there.

The Stable Relationship

Hatch in that hinterland
Which borders love and emptiness,
And that is where we live and move
And have our being.

Refugees from a warmer country,
We have no easy route back:
It is not in our gift.

A Suitable Case for Treatment

The transient and disparate forces that disrupt
the heart's rhythms can be treated.
DR KLEIN (Boston University)

Something is happening down in my pacemaker,
Something is stirring, alarming, divine,
Transient, lovely and disparate forces
Have entered my heart since your elbow touched mine.

Come and sit here and I'll show you my ECG:
My cardiologist thinks it looks fine:
But disparate forces need desperate courses,
So fly me please, darling, to see Dr Klein.

Synopsis

The lines are down between us. It's no use
To shout. We may as well
Add up the gain and loss,
Rule off the entry, and get out.

Or shall we try a new scenario?
The man preoccupied but equable;
The woman calm, but otherwise engaged,
And both of them placating, kind and fair?

Scratch under the veneer: there's more veneer.
We touched wood once, but it's no longer there.
Cry *sauve qui peut*:
New readers, start from here.

Technique

Life, you know, is set up by this great random computer,
But it has been poorly programmed.
Someone has fed in more bad news than good,
And the messages tick out mad irrelevancies and ironies.

Those putting in a modest request for comedy
Get tragedy, *tout court*:
And those banking on a touch of gravitas
Get the pratfall and the cauliflower ear.

It's no use fighting the system.
Keep a low profile, I say,
And if the messages come tapping out too black,
You can always go to earth.

Threat

The seagulls are plunging past the window.
With vixen cries they rake the ground for victims,
Ready to put the beak in.

They have not spotted me yet, here in bed,
And, with my dark coverlet and sparse hair,
I am inconspicuous.

They would like to see my face come through the door
(Disc-like, attracting harm);
But want must be their master.

My garden is their arena. They are lining the trees.
My intellect is well known to them
And they itch to pick my brains.

34

Time Slip

When she left him, time would not move on.
It hung around him, stale as city air,
Inert, refusing to get the day over.

Chores, reflections, ruses, rituals,
All failed to budge this trick of time.
He shook the clock and studied the sun.

The day had fallen into a fault,
And there he turned, suspended,
At odds: beating at the vacuum,
Shouting for a hand to pull him back
Into chronology.

Travelling Light

This whiskery old dog shed its gaze over me,
Worshipping with brown and clouded eyes,
Thinking I was God knows what:
Saviour, provider, Second Comer, dog's delight.

He was putting on the limping walk,
Currying not only favour
But commitment, love, warmth –
Who knows what package of trouble?
Soliciting, and too old for it.

I pulled back, called a halt to the affair,
Turned off round a corner, put space behind me.

I like to travel light;
And yet all day I felt trammelled:
Something grated, and distracted me
Like a broken fingernail.

Trespass

I turned to you,
Smelling out warmth like a cat,
Preying on you decorously
For touch and comfort.

We always want more than we bargain for –
The particular tone of voice,
The special intimacy,
The exclusive offer.

To appear in your mind's eye
Couched in glowing terms
And under your hand in dreams
Was my desire.

But reality was more of the commonplace.
I learned to stand in line for your largesse;
To ask for nothing, and to look for less.

Underground Car Park

*Worms can find their way through a maze
better after being fed chopped up worms
who have already learned how to do it.*
PSYCHOLOGY TEXTBOOK

How to get out?
A minotaur would be hard put to it.

Those dim, dank walls,
Those misty pillars, bald as old trees –
Glass eyes glinting between them.

Somewhere there must be a coveted egress:
Some half-lit shaft
Or bolting-tunnel.

If only the architect were fed to me
Piece by piece,
I could absorb his plan –
Quick as sugar into the bloodstream –
And appear, to applause,
Outside on the pavement.

An Uninteresting Case

The doctor looked at my palm:
'I see a reasonable life line,' he said,
'Some travel, a dark man with a glass eye

And a lovely bungalow. Take these tablets
And drop me a line about the side-effects.
Next please.' 'Wait,' I said,

'I've come about my mother, she's depressed.'
'Who isn't?' he cried, with a basilisk look,
Chewing at his frayed stethoscope,

'But this week I'm only seeing female patients
Under forty – and next week
I retire to the seaside.'

Vauxhall

Pulling through cliffs of windows
We stop at the platform:
Murky, misty; damp haloes round the lights –
The graffiti half lost in dust.

The train gives an orgasmic shudder
And falls silent.
The few passengers gaze vacantly about.
One gives a racking sigh.

Vauxhall. The word blooms in my mind,
Opening up green vistas. Down one of them
My mother, playing the piano,
Waiting for her washing to dry, and singing tremulously:
> *When Lady Betty passes by*
> *I strive to catch her bright blue eye*
> *At Vauxhall in the morning.*

Round her elbow I can just make out the words.
Her hands are crinkly from the soapsuds;
Outside, the roses catch at the blown sheets,
And in Vauxhall, it is all blossom and glances.

I smile out at the grimy wall
(*Wogs sod off – Arsenal are shit*)
And the train throbs back to life,
Sliding us on to some more ordinary place.

Vicious Circle

When I think of myself dying
My eyes fill
With sympathy for the bereaved.

Will they recover?
Will a month, a year, see them eating and sleeping again?

Well, some mourn themselves out of this world,
But often the news of death seems merely – newsworthy.

The ranks close with an indelicately hasty shuffle,
It's just a meeting of old friends at the funeral
And who's going to have the silver spoons,
And off with your boots to the Oxfam shop.

It's almost enough to make you suicidal.

Willpower

The Victorian moralists understood these things.
If you were greedy, they said,
And wished it to rain chocolates,
It would rain hard centres, and knock you down.

Well, I wished for you,
And, craving, drove to bargaining with unseen powers:
One night – or only a few hours
In return for sacrifices clearly understood,
Mortgages of future gain, promises to pay up on the nail.

Every possible resource of the will focused
As through a burning glass.

I should have remembered:
Anyone making that kind of fuss
Risks the Gods tossing down his heart's desire
And knocking him flat.

FROM **MOVING IN**

(1984)

Deadlines

Sullen, they lie in their tissue paper
refusing to speak or to move their limbs.
If they know the plot, they do not like it.

The ardent hero has lost his voice:
the incestuous father has forgotten his vice
and the heroine is in her depressive phase.

What can I do? One of them labours
into a sitting position. He cranks open his mouth
and speaks. Do you come here often? he grins.

'It's the Position That Counts'

I only have to walk down the street
past the betting shop with its rainbow door strips
and the barber's window furnished with dusty Durex;

I only have to cross the road
under the railway, where the shit-littered pavements
hint at native alsatians of fearful size;

I only have to get past the bus garage –
watching out for the sudden rush of a rogue bus
at top speed, behind schedule –

and soon I come to the Common where, in a fine dusk,
I have seen rabbits scuttle at my step, and pocket themselves
like billiard balls, into the untrammelled earth.

Occupation

A man leans in his shop doorway
In the late summer sun; arms folded;
Not much custom. People are away,
Away from the dusty suburbs.

Here the afternoons are so long...
He narrows his eyes at the indifferent traffic,
The clockwork pigeons, the shufflers
With their string bags.

He has it in him to be cool under mortar attack;
Resourceful in a sandstorm. He has it in him
To knock the Chief Librarian's wife
For six, with his Kama Sutra versatility.

After long thoughts; after scanning
The late racing results,
He feels the day turn, and subdue itself
Behind the brickwork.

In his mind a smell of beer
Forms itself, seductively.
Grinding his fag-end into the pavement
He slams down the shutters. Now, life begins.

Masters' Common Room 9 a.m.

My God, I've got the Upper Fourth first,
just when I feel like Alka Seltzer and utter hush,
and 'Yes Sir' the only spoken words,
and those whispered.

Here's the new chap – tiresomely keen
I hate him, under my smile.
I looked a bit like him
ten years ago.

Could I manage if I gave it all up,
freelanced, wrote reviews –
I've only myself to think about,
unfortunately.

Oh God, the Upper Fourth;
the late, lamented, loutish Upper Fourth.
They see in me (what I see in myself)
that I could do better.

Gardening

I've planted roseola round the door
and amenorrhoea under the window,
with a ground cover of pes planus
and spring uveitis.

Along the fence I'm training bronchiectasis
but down at the bottom it's wild
with atheroma and cystitis
and when we sit outside, the air is heady
with the blue carbuncle.

Slow Movement

Waking before dawn,
tossing over a jumble of worries,
I grope for the radio

and find a concert in full bloom. They are playing
the slow movement, and the music comes at you
straight through the chest.

On and on they play, in the empty, dusty hall,
until at last we reach a climax,
to birdsong applause.

Chairs are pushed back. A finger eases
the stiff tie from a chafed neck.
Smoke curls up round the NO SMOKING sign.

Early rays are catching the brass – and the bucket
of the first cleaner. One by one we straggle,
accelerando, into the new day.

The Accountant

Where's Jim, I ask
my briefcase winking back the morning sun.

> Round the back, past the bricks
> where the trucks park:
> past the shack with the stocks
> of the spare parts;
> down the track, through the gate
> to the waste plot –
> Jim's there.

Here he is, kneeling amongst the flowers.

This patch is a box of bloom and colour:
shake it and it would stop your breath
with rose and jasmine. There, through the leaves,
the sun strikes back light from water.
Tendrils are catching at my bowler hat
and a willow is stroking me.

But Jim, you have wasted your time here.
No wonder your figures are falling off.
Your telephone was ringing and ringing
and no one put a hand to it.
We'd better get back to the office and check out
your profit and loss:
and those letters from the bank which you buried
under the seed catalogues.

Charity

Trouble has done her good,
Trouble has stopped her trivialising everything,
Giggling too much,
Glittering after other people's husbands.

Trouble has made her think;
Taken her down a peg,
Knocked the stuffing out of her.
Trouble has toned down the vulgarity.

Under the bruises she looks more deserving:
Someone you'd be glad to throw a rope to,
Somewhere to send your old blouses,
Or those wormy little windfalls.

A Summer Afternoon

It used to take him so long
to open up: faltering footsteps,
the scrunch of chains; the tremulous key
scratching round the lock: at last a crack
for the old nose to quiver through.

That June I was busy; but in July
I knocked. Nothing stirred, only –
inside the window – great bluebottles hung,
hazed and glutted, glinting in the afternoon sun,
clotting and fringing the small panes.

A second knock dislodged a few to random motion.
Some climbed over others. There seemed to fall
a long moment of collusion:
for they did not want to come out,
and I did not want to go in.

Dreamscapes

The wind from the train sweeps the alley
which runs beside the track. It balloons my skirt

as I pedal along, and ruffles the fur
of the stout cat grooming itself by the dustbin.

Ten pairs of eyes stare from the train:
incurious; seeing, yet not seeing, the woman,

the cat, the low light which gleams on the ivy
shrouding the fence. If I were to die

round the next corner, I could still be alive
in some commuter's dream; taking a minor

and puzzling role: surfacing, perhaps, in a
garbled scene – with the ivy hiding God knows what

horror, the woman in a wheelchair, and the cat,
with the face of a near relative, smiling dreadfully.

Moving In

Well that is where the pictures hung:
Three squares; dust-rimmed and blank as a slammed door.

Were they masked, before, by Still Lives
Or scenes of Venice; or serial studies

Of an uncle coming up to bowl
In sepia white flannels; his moustache

Flaring at the batsman (off camera left)?
I forward their letters, but I do not ask.

At last it is time to mark out my territory.
I take hammer and nails; and over the squares

I superimpose my stuffed carp. Its starboard eye
Rides high, majestically, over my new room.

Coming Out

Leaning against the window,
Legs pressed languorously to the radiator,

I spot the first sign of spring
In a bleak slice of garden over the back fence.

An arm – upright as a cable-car arm –
Is trolling a duster along a washing-line,

Wiping away winter. Soon, swelling and rising
On zephyrs, the first washing is in bloom.

Loss

When at last she died
in the nursing home, where nuns
whispered along the Spanish-tiled passages,
she left a list, in shaky writing:

These are my things:
the small chair by the window,
the picture by the bed,
the blue ginger jar
and the box of photographs.

I folded the paper, laid it
in the empty ginger jar
and replaced the lid.
Some things don't bear reading twice.

II

Here in this hotel room half across the world –
the air laundered; the bathroom
shiny as a new tooth –
pain floods in at last.

No one ever did all they could:
and all we did was not enough
for you. Why couldn't you go sooner –
go when the going was good?

Not too soon. Not when you were all-powerful.
A parent owes it to a child to be in keeping:
first present; then distant; and finally
absent. But all without screaming.

Morning

After the thaw
the birds looped up through the air,
winging pale flashes in the tender light:
aspiring to something different.

After long durance, he woke one day
smiling, and could not remember why.

New Broom

Staring, square-faced at the camera
In black bombazine, they knew who they were:
Great-aunts – by the look of them –
From the cradle.

Aunt Kate was the oldest of the three
And carved out of granite.
Once she told my mother's young man
To sweep her back lawn.

She handed him a new birch-broom
But as he swept, it grew steadily shorter.
Nothing could stop it. At last
He found himself wielding a stump.

Not, evidently, a brave man,
He hot-footed it through the back gate
And sent a garbled telegram
From Paddington.

My mother never saw him again;
So my father was a different person altogether.

The Night Light on the Mantelpiece

In my dream my child was young again
and came to our room, frightened, in the night.

I lifted him on to the couch, covering him,
tucking, murmuring, love pouring down,

until I awoke, crying. It is we,
who are older, who have the real fears,

wonder who we are, cling, and need
the night light on the mantelpiece.

Scandal

Their secret affair was currency
everywhere. It passed from glass to glass
in clubs; it featured, thinly disguised,
in fiction. I had almost forgotten
the detail of it when, one night,
I saw them in a restaurant.

The lights diffused softly on his rings,
his baldness; while she – the famous hair
severely cropped – looked matrimonial,
with carrier bags. They hardly spoke.
What was there to say? We had said it all,
nibbling away at them until the teeth met bone.

Dorothy

After an illness in late middle age
Dorothy Wordsworth lost her reason.

They wheel me about. The daffodils
have come and gone, and William showed them to me.
They think my mind has also gone.
Sometimes I dream myself, in glory
and in freshness, back in Dove Cottage.
It is haunted by something which has not yet
happened. I see a crowd, a host of people.
They peer into all the corners of the life
which was mine and William's. I shout at them
as I wake. No one understands.
Mary strokes my hand, and William,
striding in from meadow, grove and stream,
reads me something from long ago.
He would tie up the beansticks then
while I baked loaves, my days
tied each to each by natural
love. There was such a time, but now
they wheel me about.

A New Scenario for the Church

Darling, I must tell you our news:
at last Stephen and I have got accepted
by the C. of E. – West London Chapter.

Of course it's going to cost a bit,
but Dora died last year and left us half
her gilts. We start with a weekend

locked in the church, with the Vicar abusing us
and making us hyperventilate and shout out
bits of the Bible. It's said to be an extremely

good start, and well worth the extra money.
You and Robert? Well I'll certainly make enquiries.
Leave it to me. Will you be around

during the summer if a sudden vacancy
turns up? What was that you said?
Oh yes of course: D.V.

Bloomsbury Snapshot

Virginia's writing her diary,
Vanessa is shelling the peas,
And Carrington's there, hiding under her hair,
And squinting, and painting the trees.

Well Maynard is smiling at Duncan,
A little to Lytton's distress,
But Ralph's lying down with a terrible frown
For he'd rather be back in the mess.

There's Ottoline, planning a party –
But Leonard's impassive as stone:
He knows that they'll all sit around in deck chairs,
Discussing their own and each others' affaires,
And forming, perhaps, into new sets of pairs:
And oh, how the bookshelves will groan.

A Luminary to Tea

At last you emerge up the station steps
Slice by slice; first the freckled cranium
Fringed with white; then the spectacles
Winking back the beaming afternoon, and now,
Complete and genial, you loom over me.
There was a hold-up on the District Line.

I draw you out on a modest tour:
This, then, is The Green
(*Very fine* – but your eye is impassive)
And here is the river bank, which is –
I falter – much painted. You look upstream
And then downstream. But I see
The river is running boringly today.
The park, also, has somehow lost its vistas
And assumed a municipal expression.

Home for tea. *No cake thank you.*
Flat as the park. I dredge up views
And old, much-trodden gossip –
But you are peering over my shoulder:
Could we watch the cricket highlights
Just for a moment? We switch hemispheres
Into a humming, electric brilliance.
A hand shoots up. A catch! The ground is
In uproar. The cat, sensing an accommodation,
Pushes its bullet head into your lap
And embarks on a long wash.

Choices
Suggested by a theme in Homecomings *by C.P. Snow*

The secret planner paces out our days:
   Beneath the margin of the conscious brain,
There is a thread that leads us through the maze.

She saw him once, and barely met his gaze,
   And hardly knew she looked for him again.
The secret planner paces out our days.

Although he meant to go – yet still he stays;
   The pattern changes, reasons are not plain,
there is a thread that leads us through the maze.

The message in the nerves; that half-heard phrase
   That forms an incantatory refrain:
The secret planner paces out our days.

So viscerally slow, the part it plays,
Its data drawn from some unknown terrain,
The secret planner paces out our days,
There is a thread that leads us through the maze.

The Maze

Hearing you cry out was one thing: finding you
was quite another. For hours I endured

the neat, woven leaves; passing and re-passing
the man with the moustache, the woman

in red, and the child with the blue balloon.
The sun rose and declined; and swifts

sent their shadows across our faces. At one time
I heard your voice. I shook the bars of the hedge then,

wrenching the branches to get through; diving
and floundering in the thicket. Straightening up

I met the eyes of the child,
who pulled her balloon close, and ran.

Self Selection

At last *Safeways*
Has made a notable contribution
To everyday philosophical thought.

SELF SELECTION is their theory, put forward
In bold caps, beside the oranges,
And who could resist it?

Who would not be pleased to carry home
A better adjusted, seamless,
Selfless self: decisive yet flexible,

Loving yet integral; cheerful
But not offensively so?
A self with poise,

58

Who knows a mot juste
From a put-down;
A complaint from a whine.

A brave self. A self
Who worries more about world starvation
Than his dandruff.

But what to do with the old self?
Drown it in a bucket? Leave it
Under the counter, where the boxes are?

It would follow you home.
You would feel it creeping back
Under your waistcoat.

It knows you hate change.

Accountability

*The musician Bruckner was handicapped by
a counting obsession which overcame him
when he was tired.*

Life is wearing me down
by a process of attrition, multiplication
and unnecessary movement –
largely on the part of birds.

The number of windows in the street
is easily achievable: furrows in a field,
berries on a branch. The thirty seven roses
on my counterpane are unequivocal.

But the swallows make my heart race
with their terrible interweaving:
and what I dread is a clear sky
at night. Always at dusk,
I am drawn to the window. Reluctantly
I turn my face upwards.

Last Words

How he loved the bird.
Each day, between his duties with the large mammals
he would come to its cage.

The bird clung to the mesh,
powerful and black: its tool-sharp beak
working at the metal.

Little by little, the keeper's few words
lodged in its brain. One day
the feathers at its throat moved

and a gruff ventriloquist voice
spoke from its beak:
'How's the old boy then?'

The keeper didn't hear.
Last week he'd been retired, after a mauling –
Been sent off to Perth, to his one relation.

He never recovered. The bird,
fixing its listeners with a glittering eye,
uttered its question time and time again.

Need

See the fledgling cuckoo
lording it, like a blackmailing lodger.
He is all beak. The small birds
dart and shuttle, mad to feed him.

If an alien child, hungry and rapacious,
fixed itself to a woman's breast,
would she nurse it? Need is an undertow
that pulls us against our will.

Tidying Up

Hear the shots at dawn.
Multiple murders are taking place
Of a sensible kind:
The culling of the deer.

Animals seen limping
May not walk again;
Animals which falter and fall
Need not apply to rise.

In principle I approve of this principle.
Such neatness and utility. Why can't we practise it?

My head itches where the metal would enter.

Survivors

Anyone could batter down the ferns
with their weak, suppliant fronds unfurling
and bending to the prevailing wind. In dry weather
fire wipes out whole acres of them.

But under your feet the new shoots are
inexorable. Bumping up, hard as beads,
they fist into hooks, into question marks,
putting on meekness all over the earth.

Postcards

The postcards flock
and settle on my doormat.

The seas are so blue
you could dip your pen in them;

villas are heavy with vines,
nothing interrupts the sun.

'All we do is eat, drink
and laze on the beach.'

But now, the spiders are trapezing
across the late asters;

travellers wander back
through airport lounges

with their miscellaneous bags,
their brown feet.

I feed the postcards
into the first fire of winter.

Blue skies darken,
villas crumble; bodies jerk

and fold. In no time
they are ash.

Perspectives

When it comes to rewriting the past
we are all into faction:

last week's faux pas can be re-choreographed,
last month's extravagance taken in to fit:

and last year's love affair totally edited –
the roles re-cast, the story line strengthened

and one's own part adapted and rendered
more rational. Darker areas of betrayal and folly

are lost, with clever lighting
and the use of perspective.

All it takes is time, rehearsal
and one's own gullibility.

Short Story

As I knocked the cup from the shelf
my mind flashed up reprises:

that glass you dropped, the dark hotel room,
my letter in the rack, your car driving away;

a masterpiece of précis.
The cup hits the floor. I turn to pick up the pieces.

Mutability

Some months after it was finished
(the raw emotions concreted over)
she saw him again, and was amazed at the change.

Surely he was shorter by at least an inch;
coarser at the neck and waist;
the endearing imperfections overtly more imperfect
and less endearing; why had he changed so much
since she stopped loving him?

She smiled in condescending sympathy:
but then, so did he.

Chance Meeting

Are we the same people –
All that love and rancour
Dried up and crumbled away?

Now we smile, ask after the children,
Pour cups of tea where once we threw them.
The antic hay has danced us all apart.

We hardly recognise old partners,
Or remember the music that sent us round
Yearning for the wrong hand.

The Innocent

'If only she would come back,' he said,
'Everything would be all right.'

What the innocent can't see
are the "if onlys" just over the horizon,
spawning and feeding
and forming into sub-groups
of want and desire.

For a moment he thinks he's made it –
but 'Look behind you,' we cry
'Look behind you.'

C

Cookery

Strange how the heat both softens and hardens:
Turning sinews to gelatine
And liquid batters into crispness and substance
Or cricket-bat solidity.

Soon, I will take you and feed you
My stew. It will be thick, reddish brown,
And rich as the beginning of the world.
In it will be dark mouthfuls engorged with wine,
Crusted and melded with gold and amber tenderness.

Rumour of it will reach you from the kitchen,
Embarrassing you with saliva –
But when you eat, I shall leave the room,
For you must be alone to commune
With this dark tide, which will flood,
Like evangelism, through the blood
Under your pale accountant's skin.

Later, I will sit with you over crumbly meringues
And you will smile, under the pearls on your moustache.

Such goodness. I know it is right.
You will soften and harden for me.

Is It Anything to Worry About, Doctor?

Oh no, nothing to worry about.
We all have to go in the end. Some of us
Would envy you. Better the quick coup
Than the messy loiter. Do what you like.
Just put your affairs in order.
There's nothing much to worry about – and soon
Nothing at all.

A Moment of Distraction

The water, molten and opaque,
Looks fit to lie down on.

From the bridge I can see
Two figures to the side of the landscape
Doing something on the foreshore, in waders.

An urban river, cliffed in
With square-shouldered buildings
And rusting machinery. Trees on the towpath
Festooned with rubbish from high tide.

The water looks resilient.
I think you could lie down on it.

Some men are working on the parapet.
'Come on duck,' one calls,
'Don't do it today. We fished two out yesterday
And it's not in our contract.'

He throws down a stone
And the water swallows it neatly.

I hurry on. It looks like rain.

Below the Surface

This is reparation for something imperfectly
remembered, but rooted here. The lolling willows,

the silver shallows, all formed a part of it.
I look up. The water boatmen scurry round the lilies.

There is the meniscus, echoing the curve
of the eyeball; also the curve to the horizon.

Under my back, the river gravel, my bed and board
and shelf life; and here am I, victim

of my average weekly yearnings, so peaceful now
as all the curves darken, one by one, in harmony.

CENTRAL RESERVATIONS

DAILY ROUND

Clay Pipes

Here is the box with the pieces of clay pipe,
stems like twigs, bowls swagged and ribbed,
all cracked and chipped; but neatly docketed
in your schoolboy hand.

They were difficult to spot on the river bank
amongst the pebbles. We spent hours
bent over like ancients, quartering the ground
(you in your first adolescence, me in my second).

The Thames mud smelled of beer from the brewery;
fishermen stood peacefully in their waders,
while we scrunched and scraped and pounced
with nervous absorption.

When two pieces jigsawed together
you gave your special, satisfied frown.

Addictions

We're all hooked on something:
gold or pinchbeck;
solitude; a particular pain,
the soft option
or something harder.

Kick one habit and,
as you stand quietly at the window,
another will dust down that empty chair
and settle in.

72

Bed

In this store window, a vast bed,
radiant white in satin, lace and crystals,
embowered, flounced and veiled: a Swan Lake –
an iced cake of a bed; unsullied, intacta.

It knows nothing of body fluids,
amorous heats, night sweats,
birthings, couplings, dyings –
such leaky businesses.

By this bed, a lover would kneel,
slender as a freesia, his samite cuff
trailing the floor. Could you relish
so immaculate a conception?

Central Reservations

I've just been taught another damn lesson.
Is there no end to them?

It's still all life tests,
crossroad decisions, multiple choices.

Even last words may be subject to assessment:
but do we have faith in the examiner?

As I ponder this, a voice issues
from clouds looming above the window:

Trust me, it booms, *we know what I am doing.*

August in the Offices

The small divorces of the summer offices
relieve the year, let in the air.

Absentees sun themselves by succulent hedgerows
or sit in rain-soaked reveries on river banks –

but their desks gather accretions; the names on their doors
have a distant, commemorative look.

Territories suffer encroachment, feuds and flirtations
lose their fine balance; but in September –

the canvas shoes flung to the back of the cupboard –
flocks of fresh memos gather for the winter.

The Claimant

There's no reasoning with gloom:
it breaks out from below the pavement
into your head, into the corners of the room.

Supposing you trace its lineage. What's the point?
Name it; it merely answers
You're the one I want.

One's Correspondence

I wrote to you to say that I'd be there
but lost the letter giving your address
and now I cannot find it anywhere.

Although I've searched until I'm in despair,
what's worrying me most is, I confess,
I wrote to you to say that I'd be there.

It came first thing on Tuesday (to be fair
the breakfast table was in quite a mess)
and now I cannot find it anywhere.

I think you said you lived in Berkeley Square
or did you say you'd moved to Inverness?
I wrote to you to say that I'd be there.

Where parties are concerned, you have a flair.
The letter said: 'Please come in fancy dress,'
and now I cannot find it anywhere.

I'm sure I wrote a note but couldn't swear
to posting it: this is an S.O.S. –
I wrote to you to say that I'd be there
and now I cannot find it anywhere.

Compassion

Waiting in the supermarket queue
with my mange-tout and steak,
I gazed abstractedly
at the shoes of the woman in front –

plastic and misshapen, sticking plaster
where one rubbed at the instep.
In her basket (her hands grey and knuckly)
some small bony meat.

She looked so illimitably patient and hopeless
that the easy tears blurred my eyes at the cash desk.
But then I went home again,
and I was so busy with my dinner party, you see.

Confession

One day, she told a stranger on a train
everything. After twenty years
she didn't find it easy to begin,
but then, encouraged by his faint, grey nods,

she fitted words together:
explanations, revelations, vindications –
the relief was enormous.
She touched her face with cambric, feeling shriven.

At the next station he rose, creakingly,
'So very nice to chat with you, but I fear
the conversation was a shade one-sided.
This wretched deafness...'

76

Problem One

After a wedding, ten people
stay the night in a house
which has one W.C.

At 9 a.m. the hostess administers
150 ml. tea to each person,
and all sip at the rate of 50 ml. per minute.

90% of the guests then fall to planning
a furtive sortie to the W.C. – not wishing to attempt
fur-tongued, half naked pleasantries en route.

The protagonists crouch anxiously
behind their door-jambs, like characters
in an early French ciné-melodrama,

struggling to interpret
the creak of the floorboards,
the click of a door-catch.

Suddenly, a youth downstairs
staggers from a sofa, pulls on jeans,
plods up the stairs to the W.C.

and locks himself in. He takes from his pocket
a copy of Camus' *The Plague*, and settles down
for a good read.

Ladies at Lunch

Do you remember his hand was shaking
like this? Mine too, Elena,
but you were always brave.

'You first Maria,' he said to me,
and I held the needle over the flame.
I don't think we tried to sterilise the cork.

What innocents we were. How deliciously
he shocked us: 'Of course this is only a metaphor
for sexual penetration.'

He kept stroking the cat absent-mindedly
and having to wash his hands all over again.
I thought we'd be there all night.

'Let's get on with it,' I said,
'or my parents will be back.'
I lay back in the chair and clamped my eyes shut.

When I bled all over two linen napkins
he went very white. He was much keener
on sex than on ear piercing

but he hoped that one thing would lead
to the other. Which in time it did,
in that bed-sit of his – so bohemian,

all lino and frayed edges.
We were both foolish, Elena,
but at least I didn't let him marry me.

Heaven on Earth

The loveliest times in all my life
my mother told me – near the end of it –
were when I used to go to the Caledonian Market
on Tuesday mornings. I remembered her
coming home on those Tuesdays,
ruffled, animated, as from an assignation
or triumph. Once she brought back
a clockwork canary in a wire cage
which sang on two notes and gyrated
like a tiny feather duster.
When it dropped off its perch
she took it back to the stall
quivering with delicious indignation
and had it put miraculously right.
In those days, she sighed,
anything could be made better.

Monochrome

I want so much to find this empty room;
the quiet light striking the bed into eminence
against the shadowed walls.
No view. No one calls.
It is a retreat. Yet I would not pray there
but lie between cool sheets
watching the reflection of flowers,
pale in their white jar.

Diversions

In old age, confined to bed,
my mother developed a keen obsession.

Lorry jack-knifed on the M4, she would cry
as you skirted the commode to greet her:

*They'll have to leave at Exit 2
and go round here* – she had a map

on her bedside table:
her thin finger quivered.

Our small talk, our flowers and chocolates
washed up against a tide

of burst water mains, spillages,
contraflows. We nodded solemnly.

She'd gained a nourishing rapport
with all the road junctions in the country.

Are you sorry you never travelled?
I asked her. She shook her head

at my stupidity. Every day,
every night, she travelled.

Trouble Ahead

In the taxi, in a sweating, static
jam, you check your watch again.
Your train! You're bound to miss it.
And what about the stranger
who is meeting you? Troubled scenarios
blossom and race through your head.

Someone leans on his horn, and the hooting
spreads, like an animal cry
through a herd. A bearded man
strides back angrily from some crisis point
ahead. *Christ, can't you wait a few minutes.*
Someone's dead.

All fall silent
but it's an exasperated silence.
Death buggers up the traffic no end.
People should die in bed.

Choice

You're the one I boned up mah jongg for
You're the one I bought the chaise longue for
You're the one I yearn to go wrong for.

You're the one I'll garden my plot with
You're the one I'll throw in my lot with
You're the one I'll find my G spot with.

You're the one I've had my teeth capped for
You're the one my scruples were scrapped for
You're the one I get all unwrapped for:
                            You're the one.

Don't Look Now

Today, I have been seeing
stairparts. It is best
not to look directly
at the heavy duty fixers,
the two-gang pattresses (japanned
and countersunk) or the sinisterly named
door knob set with escutcheons.

The togglers, with their rising butts
and easy-on hinges, were hanging around
as usual, waiting for straight couplings
and high performance cavity screws;
but the white-faced hardboard lay
motionless and epoxy: it was
sashlocked to the roundheads.

Entrails

*I am convinced that digestion is the great
secret of life –*
REV. SYDNEY SMITH

Twenty-two feet of wonders
Twenty-two feet of woes:
Why we're obliged to have so many yards of them
Nobody really knows.

Sometimes they lie retentive,
Sometimes they're wild and free,
Sometimes they writhe and get madly expulsive
The moment you're out to tea.

Entrails don't care for travel,
Entrails don't care for stress:
Entrails are better kept folded inside you
For outside, they make a mess.

Entrails put hara-kiri
High on their list of hates:
Also they loathe being spread on the carpet
While someone haruspicates.

Twenty-two feet of wonders
Twenty-two feet of woes:
Why we're obliged to have so many yards of them
Nobody really knows.

Moscow Spring

In the Kuskova gardens
workmen lift the wooden boxes
from the delicate statues.

Tender bushes are unwrapped
from their overcoats; twigs unbend
in the melting light.

The men warm to their work;
hang their fur hats
in a row on the fence.

Games

A rat with his head in a tin
enjoys low tide. The river has exposed
its flanks of mud and shingle:

tusks of wood at the water's edge
speak of mammoths or great amphibians
but here on the path we pick our way

through artefacts – expanded polystyrene
chunky as peppermint toffee; string
elaborately knotted; an old bald

broom. Joggers thud past miming
all degrees of anguish; but the gulls
have landed in a drift on the water

and are rocking in a trance up and down,
up and down, on the wash
from the pleasure steamer.

Faidagery

Three men in camel overcoats – coarse, moon-faced,
slicked-back hair – are sitting in the front row
of an audience.

They mutter to each other disapprovingly
then rise, button their coats
and ostentatiously leave, saying:

'I can't stand to see women committing
Faidagery.'

It's not in the dictionary: I look for it
when I wake up. But it might be in some
arcane tome or medical compendium.

One could be committing Faidagery
in all innocence.
There is always something you do
which annoys somebody.

Jessie's Bakery

This shop, something of a cult with local inhabitants
for its delicious hot bread, was closed by the health
authorities on the grounds that the flour was full of moths.

Blindfold, you could find it by the reek
of stale cats. Big Jessie queens it here, her grey hair
dollied up in yellow curls, six days a week.

It takes her years to talk your loaf into a bag.
The weather never tires of hearing about itself.
Flour stirs and settles; hours lag.

In fact, time stops. Flies, as if in amber,
stiffen in syrup tarts. Sultanas scab
the shelves; the customers half remember

the world, in its complexity and pain;
and, like the lotus eaters, grow averse
to facing it again.

Frank's Journal, December 1878

That morning, it was wonderfully cold.
I put a bowl of water on the sill
and in an hour it froze. So far, so good.

The dog-cart picked me up at half past eight,
then we collected Willie, Jack and Fred
and up we went to Earith. By the time
we started off for Welney, it was ten.

My first long run on skates. They went ahead
while I got in my stride with less despatch.
My face ached from the wind: I had to rest
by Bedford's, but I soon warmed to my work
and got to Welch's Dam by half past twelve:
the last six miles took only half an hour.

The Welney skaters – fastest in the world –
were marvellous to watch, and there were crowds
to cheer them on. The low rays of the sun
struck sparks of fiery light from skates and ice.

At the Blue Boar we ate a pigeon pie
and, taking biscuits and a flask of tea,
we turned for home again, against the wind.

We ran eight miles and rested by the Dam,
then down the counter wash, across the bank
and round by Hundred Foot, where just before
a lad had drowned (but no one that we knew).

We passed the Dinsdale boys on Bury Fen...
and after that I slowed, and lagged behind.
My legs were made of lead, my hands of ice;
the sun had disappeared, the sky was dark;
I prayed for strength to make myself keep on.

I can't remember how I reached my goal
but Lansdowne James was standing on the bank.

He pulled me from the ice, but I could move
no more: my skates were frozen to my feet
completely, so he took me on his back
and carried me to shelter. Such a day!

I offered prayers of thanks, and was so bold
as to petition that the ice should hold.

Wants

Like yours, my wants are simple:
security with the window ajar,

the battle without the spilt guts;
the family to throw off

and rediscover: a magical bed-post
and Life Everlasting, with my own teeth.

THE STRONGER SEX

The Badminton Game

That morning, I awoke and went down
just as I was, in my green slippers,
to look at the hydrangea mariesii –
the only flower Clifton allows in the garden,
for he must have his trees and shrubs.

Out I crept, my slippers darkening in the dew,
and hearing a movement beside me
I turned and found Ruth. She was carrying
the racquets; and so – smiling, not speaking –
we ran between the great bushes to the net,

and there we played (quietly, of course,
so that Uncle Edward might not hear)
until the breakfast gong recalled us.
We ran up the backstairs en deshabille,
and down the front ones, decorous but tardy,

and kissed Uncle Edward; but I took care
to embrace him as he likes best, to forestall
reproof. Colour rose up behind his moustache
and his face worked silently, but then he vanished
as usual, behind *The Times*.

She's Nothing But Trouble

If she smiles, don't smile back.
But of course you will, like an electrician
taking chances with the wiring
on a dull Tuesday afternoon.

90

Albert Memorial

Passing the Albert Memorial
I remember our night of love, so-called,
which started with a concert, and went on

to the expensive hotel where we ate our supper –
too much, too rich, too noisy –
the violinist, with his pander leer

fingering and bowing over the stuffed avocados
and I, like (but unlike) a Vestal Virgin
wishing I were home at my sacred hearth.

Courage! Courage! This is what is called Life.
Put down the hermit's dish and tackle
this hunk of meat – so vigorous

it nearly leaps out of its sea of sauce.
At last we are in the lift which elevates
from Gluttony to Lust. The corridors stretch

into infinity; such luxurious cells
and here by the bed is a Gideon Bible.
I open it, keen for guidance or diversion.

Too late! You bend over me,
tall as the Albert Memorial, or a tree,
take the book and tidy it away,
bored with the prologue and ready for the play.

Terribly Weak. Please Come.

Darling Mama. The hamper came today,
I never got such a jolly surprise.
But the shirts are Willie's. Mine are
one quite scarlet, and the other lilac.

* * *

A delightful viva voce, first in the Odyssey,
where we discussed epic poetry in general,
dogs and women...Of course I knew
I had got a First, so I swaggered
horribly. My poor mother is in great delight.

* * *

I want to be one of Her Majesty's
Inspectors of Schools. Will you
write me a testimonial?

* * *

My name is printed six feet high –
printed, it is true, in those
primary colours against which
I spend my life protesting, but anything
is better than virtuous obscurity.

I am perfectly happy, and hope
you will be very fond of my wife.

The baby is wonderful.
It has a superb voice,
its style is essentially Wagnerian.

We must wear cloaks with lovely linings. Otherwise
we shall be very incomplete.

* * *

I am much better. I go every day
and drive in a beautiful forest called
the Bois de Boulogne, and in the evening
I dine with my friend. I hope
you are taking great care of dear Mamma.

*　*　*

After the play is produced
I leave for the South of France
where I am obliged to go
for my health.

*　*　*

Bosie has insisted on stopping here
for sandwiches. He is quite like a narcissus,
so white and gold.

I hope you will enjoy my play. It is written
by a butterfly for a butterfly.

*　*　*

Dearest of all boys,
you must not make scenes with me.
They kill me. They wreck
the loveliness of life.

*　*　*

Dearest Robbie: Since I saw you, something has happened.

*　*　*

Inform the Committee of the Albemarle
that I resign my membership.

*　*　*

As I sit here in this dark cell
I blame myself.

You had no motives in life.
You had appetites merely.

* * *

The idea that he is wearing anything I gave him
is peculiarly repugnant to me.

* * *

The abscess has been running now
for the entire time of imprisonment.

* * *

As for my clothes, my fur coat
is all I need really. The rest
I can get abroad.

Heath was my hatter, and understands my needs.

* * *

My life was unworthy of an artist: now I hope
to do some work.

* * *

Of course I love you more than anyone else
but our lives are irreparably severed.

* * *

It is impossible for us to meet.

* * *

Everyone is furious with me
for going back to you
but they don't understand us.

* * *

I am sorry…but what is there in my life
for which I am not sorry?

I do think that, if we engage not to live together,
I might still be left the £3 a week.

The morgue yawns for me.
I go and look at my zinc bed there.

                  *   *   *

Friday and Saturday I had not a penny
and had to stay dinnerless in my room.

                  *   *   *

How I used to toy with that tiger, Life.

                  *   *   *

I made great friends with a young
Seminarist. He said he would not
forget me, and I do not think
he will, for every day
I kissed him, behind
the High Altar.

                  *   *   *

I have now been in bed for ten weeks.
The expenses of my illness amount
almost to £200.

                  *   *   *

TERRIBLY WEAK. PLEASE COME.

Tête-à-Tête

After supper (ratatouille, heated on his gas ring)
she remarked on a moth which circled the lamp
throwing wild shadows round the room.

When it quivered to rest on the rubber plant
they leafed through his book of lepidoptera
their knees almost touching,

they-leaned over its furry, palpitating body,
their heads almost touching, and at last,
after an awkward pause,

he read aloud: *The Monarch butterfly*
knocks the female to the ground
and copulates with her wherever she falls.

Almost at once, she looked at her watch and,
murmuring politely, slipped from the door
and flew down the steps to the street.

Bottleneck

The bottleneck
in her journey home that night
was the down escalator at Knightsbridge.

He chose to wait there,
looking upwards
for her clocked black stockings,
the red flared skirt,
the swinging plait.

When she saw him
she turned back in a flash,
climbing, stumbling,
passing and re-passing
the bra-and-pantie girl
with her languorous glance
and her cleavage
       cleavage
       cleavage

The Winner

As a rival he was unassailable:
eating from her fingers,
lounging on her bed,
canvassing attention
with his upturned, obscene,
bald stomach.

When at last I despatched him
he lay, mingling his pelt
with the hearthrug,
unmoving but complacent,
knowing that his last gasp
was the coup de grâce.

D

Bargaining

He wakes to his old obsession.
Nothing has changed.

He will trawl the streets
as usual, for a chance meeting;

he will plead, as usual
with her answering machine.

But in a flash revelation
he knows what is needed:

a sacrifice. Unknown powers
must be placated.

He polishes his car,
drives to the waste ground

behind the Odeon. There
he sets fire to it.

His second love is immolated
to gain his first.

Necessary sadness; a cleansing
blaze. Ash settles

in his thinning hair.
The tears are a relief.

He turns towards her house. His ear
anticipates the joyous peal

of her doorbell:
her cry of surrender.

On Lake Como

I expected nothing in return;
or very little. My negotiated role
was avuncular. I paid the hotel bills,
gave him a few lire, saw that he had
a good time. I swallowed back instruction,
edification, passion.
                    I was afraid
that the mountains would bore him,
or the formality of the gardens,
prinked out amongst the cypresses and
balustrades. We rode the steamer on the lake
by day, kept on the move, kept eating
the coloured ices and drinking the red wine,
glass after glass, until the land rocked
round the lake, and he grew languorous –
but never pliable.

One evening, at a table by the jetty,
the wind suddenly blew cold over the water
and I turned and put my arms round him.
For a moment he did not draw back.
That was all. I lay awake until dawn.

Chacun

'That weekend, she lay on the bed
as usual, smooth and distant in my arms.
We seemed set for our normal parts –
I, noisy, active, verging on the hysterical;
she marmoreal, abstracted
among the rucked and musky sheets.

And then, this day, she moved:
her body moved to me.
Her teeth clenched, a tremor broke in her
like power through a fault in the earth.

I swung over, hot as fur, and fought her
to conclusion. We did not speak.
If I laughed, it was only briefly:
but when I left, she slammed the door on me,
lock, hook and bolt.'

Leaving Jenkins
(extracts from the diary of a young schoolmaster in 1876)

Sunday

As I had no timepiece, my own
being at the menders, I got up late.

A typical Sunday: the Iron Church in the morning,
Sunday School this afternoon (the boys unruly

both in Jenkins' class and in my own);
a capital sermon this evening.

100

Tuesday

Tomorrow I shall have been on this earth
for 21 years. I have resolved, with God's help,

to give a better account of myself within the next year,
if spared. Walked to Finsbury Park with Jenkins.

Tonight I am reading Pepys' Diary. He seems a man
utterly devoid of real, sound principles.

Wednesday

Received three letters on my birthday,
from my mother, my father and Fred.

Took singing in the Senior Room
while Mr Timpson examined my class in dictation.

Jenkins is suffering from indigestion. Went with him
to Dr Hill, who charged him 1/6d. and told him nothing.

Saturday

Went to look at the Great Eastern terminus.
It is very tastily got up.

This evening, Mr Sherlock from upstairs
brought down his galvanic battery,

vacuum tubes, microscope and organ accordion.
Talked until 2 a.m. Other lodgers displeased.

Saturday

To Beavis to be measured for a suit
of summer clothes (55/-). Jenkins ordered a waistcoat.

At last made up my mind to see Henry Irving
in *The Bells*. Felt better for it –

if all theatres were carried on like this,
there would be little harm done.

Sunday

The sermon this morning dealt with
vicarious sacrifice: discussed with Jenkins.

Tonight, the Rev. Marmaduke Millar told us
why he believed in angels; it was quite scientific.

So tired, I rode home in a public vehicle
though I cannot think it right on a Sunday.

Saturday

To the City to see the progress
of the Metropolitan Railway.

My face was much swollen from the wind
and the druggist gave me camomile flowers,

poppy heads and a black draught.
Jenkins came round this evening and read to me.

Thursday

I am accepting the post at Woodhurst School
at £80 plus £5 as Clerk of the Board.

Jenkins is sorry that I am going.
I believe I have done him good:

I have tried to instil in him
a taste for literature, and he has taken

to the Popular Educator; but he wonders
what he will do when I have gone.

SEEING THINGS

Seeing Things

Suddenly, the pool is alive
with small boys; they weave
and wriggle, slippery as tadpoles,
until they are summoned to order
down at the shallow end.

I make a decorous turn
in the deeper water,
and something catches my eye
far below. A child-like figure
is spreadeagled at the bottom of the pool.
I try to scream, but water
fills my mouth.

The figure drifts, in slow motion,
towards the side – I follow
dumb with fear, heart knocking,
ready to grasp at hair, at limbs:

it blooms upwards, growing like magic
and comes out of the water
as a burly, bearded man,
who heaves himself up the steps,
checks his watch, and turns,
placidly, towards the high board.

History

Some changes come so slowly:
nothing happens, yet something is happening.

The boy is on a slow dissolve into youth.

104

The creeper covers the pergola
though you sat under it for days
and not a leaf moved.

Her heart cools to you perhaps
but when did this begin –

was it that day when her gaze
strayed to someone for a moment;

or when she first moved her hand
away, like this?

Fun on the Beach

There are three of us in this poster.
The one at the back, wild with laughter
and trying to keep up, is me.

As usual, two girls and a man
are running hand-in-hand along the shore:
gold sand, white foam, blue sea.

She's the one in front, mane flying,
nipples erect. His brown legs race like pistons.
He wants to wrestle her into the sand.

So frivolous we are, so free, so tanned!
As instructed, I am showing my teeth
and clinging to his cold, reluctant hand.

If You Come

The birds come to feed me. Yesterday
one brought bread and today I have a nut, a snail
and a berry, red as your mouth.

Moving air sighs in the eaves:
La belle indifférence I hear, as nightfall
robs the trees of a dimension.

Messages, of course, I disseminate freely:
one behind the clock, one in the knife drawer,
one into my letterbox – an oubliette in its own right.

If you come, take the aerial route,
alighting near the embankment
where the backless cupboards and bony umbrellas

are all pierced through with heartsease and dock,
branches strive through the brickwork
and the paving is grouted with moss.

In the Summerhouse

In the summerhouse
you cannot hear your children crying.

Plaintive sounds fan out
from the far windows

and dissipate into the canopy of trees.
Everything loosens in the heat,

petals, buds, muslin.
Hands unpin your hair...

now you hear nothing,
but the tick of a watch.

The Last Great Fog

The fog came down at four,
thick and impassive at the windows,
and suddenly the office was an island.

You walked me home through this strangeness.
The buses had given up. An occasional car
faltered along the road, its lights describing
swirling cylinders of nothingness.

The fog set us free. We laughed at everything.
We were abroad, unattached, in lunatic spirits:
we clung, falling about on kerbstones.
You pulled me inside your overcoat
and the tweed tasted of fog.

The next day dawned bathetically fine.
You worked without remission at your desk
and I at mine.

Puzzle Picture

Here is a puzzle picture. It is a garden:
flowers, ferns, a tree, a bush.
In it are hidden a man, a woman and a child.

The artist is so cunning with his brush.
Is that a woman up there in the tree
or merely a strange configuration of the boughs?

Perhaps she is gazing down through the lush
foliage, to where a man's hand
seems to be touching a freckled knee,

or can she see two figures lying
oddly intertwined; plaits tied in ribbon bows,
a smiling mouth half hidden by a leaf?

One thing is certain, somebody is crying.
Tears fall from the tree into the quivering ferns.
We cannot call it rain – unless rain burns.

Waking in the Garden

I think I know where I am.
A rumbling train shivers the ants in the grass,
a branch shifts and groans,
my cheek is creased
by a rug of folded hills.

I cannot make my eyes open.

Someone may be near me.
A voice cries 'havoc' –
but who would use such a word?
My heart knocks – the only part of me
which can move.

A doll I had once
would not open her eyes;
her blind lids were shellac pink
and blank as insolence.
We punished and punished her.

In the silver distance
glasses ring with laughter.
Music spools out of a window
and is pulled back in again.
I concentrate my will –

prise open a crack of light
which falls on the yolk of a daisy,
on the mountainous pores of my arm,
on a gargantuan hand
which flexes itself in the grass.

Lost Belongings

The preamble was brilliantly put together:
the downland path leading to the horizon
under fresh snow; a spaniel running back to us
with a stick. We bend towards him, and as we walk on
you take my hand in yours. A close-up shows
my shocked delight. But the face
is strangely unlike my own.

We are seen growing closer. The theatre seats
at your own play; my friends becoming envious;
the first kiss, in that shadowy room
with the blue chairs. We seem set
for a life of bliss and press coverage

until I awake from this grotesque miscasting,
cooling down from euphoria to my real self.

It must have been someone else's dream
drifting in the ether, attaching itself
to the wrong night's sleep – like a video
from the wrong box, viewed by mistake
but with serendipitous delight.

Modus Vivendi

Each night, as he played patience
she stood behind his shoulder.

'Jack on Queen,' she would cry
just before he spotted it himself.

How was it, then, that she murdered him
rather than the reverse?

Some games have rules
which are the very devil to understand.

Thrush

On the first day
the thrush lay in the gutter
stiffening, its legs crossed
as in entrechat.

On the fourth day
its limbs were as skewed
as a broken umbrella frame.

On the eighth day
it was an old brown rag,
stained and frayed.

On the tenth day
it came back into focus
pressed flat – presenting,
by chance, an austere bas-relief
of itself in flight.

Revelations

Last night, I dreamed a dream
of such significance
that, symbol by metaphor, I unpicked it
and understood the mistakes of the past:
the deceptions, the mistimings,
the mysterious intractabilities
of the heart.
                    Unfortunately
it came rather late –
being of potential value
only if we are scheduled to go round again
on the same circuit.

Visiting Time

In the ward, after the stroke,
he could not remember whom he liked
and whom he disliked.

A young man with reddened eyes
held his hand. He could not name him
though the tie seemed familiar.

When a woman swept in with flowers
and seemed to assume intimacy
he feigned sleep.

The Slipping Glimpse

I am into the business
of uninvention.

My desk is loaded with applications:
I am quite private behind my in-tray.

The procedures, you can imagine
are tortuous: the paperwork, the manual work,

the research, the lasering out of information
from human brain cells.

Often there are misunderstandings
about my scope and capability:

(Famine? Disease?
I do not set myself up against God.)

My prime achievements would mean nothing to you –
success conceals success.

You may hear a phrase, perhaps,
cut off from its context –

muffled sounds on the radio of a passing car;
words heard through a door as it closes.

Hour by Hour

The number of hours in stock for each of us
is tiresomely finite. Stamped
and docketed, they grin up at you
from the shelves of the cellar
where it is too dark to count.

How to use the ones at the front
is the first problem: frighteningly they melt away –
in bus queues, in adversarial dramas over drains;
in sleeping things off. Sometimes someone
scoops up their whole shelf-full and throws them
out of the window, murmuring
'It's the only language they understand.'

Your Laugh

Your laugh, wide and benign enough
to swallow the world.

No one laughing like that
can protect themselves against attack.

The sofa shakes its sides in sympathy.
Smiles bud out round the room.

Your arching, glinting, risky laugh.

114

ATTACHMENTS

Cut and Thrust

A man much younger than yourself, personable, smiling,
falls into close conversation with you at a party.

His shoulders block off the room – his eyes widen politely
when you recite the ages of your children.

He touches your sleeve, fills your glass,
reads your palm. Ancient machinery,

fitful and reluctant, starts up inside you,
whirrs. You fan yourself a little.

A stir of introductions separates you;
but he returns to breathe some gossip into your ear.

When you are leaving, coming down the stairs,
searching out your car keys,

he is standing in the hall looking up.
'Goodnight,' you say, but he doesn't answer;

and he beckons, smiling his personable smile,
to the blonde girl in sequins behind you.

Caller

Why does she allow it?
She looks down with distaste
at his vulgar brown curls,
his red pointed tongue slipping in and out
over the blue vein in the curve
of her arm. The clock nags; the air
suffocates with carnations.

116

In the middle of a resolve
to run from the room, she leans back
to catch her breath, and slides her feet
out of her purple slippers.

His tongue begins to travel.

My Sister

She was the first to hold her own spoon
        the first to amuse the uncles
        the first to wear the pink tulle dress.

She was the first to get a Valentine
        a wedding bouquet
        a child.

She was the first to have a fur coat
        the first to sit on a committee
        the first to say no to mother.

She was the first to have a bad prognosis
        a walking frame
        a hired nurse.

She is the first to have a coffin.

At last we draw level.

Dear Mother

I can't put my finger on it
but he's acting silent
and typing out lists of grievances.

On the boat he stood me near the rail
and told me: *lean over,*
look down at the fish.

Now he's booking our vacation.
The brochure shows cliff paths, deep seas,
lonely islands.

Don't worry he sometimes says
if Fate should come between us.
We can meet again on the other side.

'It's Up to You'

'When he's in a rage – teeth glinting
through the beard (which I want to touch),
eyes as hot as boiled marbles,
it's like walking on the edge of murder:
I know that game.

Once, when I was three
my mother left me in the kitchen,
a sharp knife on the table.
Be a good girl. Don't touch the knife.

I wrapped my finger in my skirt
and watched the red soak through.
I liked it. You don't have to cry.
It's up to you.'

118

Mutual Assured Destruction

Once they would eat from the same plate –
fat black cherries, millefeuilles,
mouthfuls of fragrant melon.

It was always Tea for Two in those days,
but slowly the taste turned bitter;
the songs slurred into silence.

Now, he sleeps in the basement
and her bed is locked upstairs, the sheets
stiff, right-angled, unyielding.

The solicitors have the matter in hand.
Thick white envelopes
tongue through the letterbox.

At post time, they hover in the hall
at the edges of neutral territory,
awaiting despatches.

Fountains

Afterwards, they compare their favourite words:
parabola, brumous, jasmine, watershed.

The window brightens, admits
the two-tone wail of the dustcart.
Darling, didn't Einstein have a good word too?
Something sibilant?...Yes, do that.

Lust is so moist: those little fountains.
Cheap flights. See Versailles and die.
Who knows what great drought may lie ahead?

The Letter

I read your letter: then I took a knife
and went into the garden. There was much
that needed doing: everything in leaf
and flower, grossly intertwined; each branch

a mess of sappy green. I pruned the vine
until the twitching stalks lay in a pile.
I pulled the red camellia blossoms down
and ground them into fragments with my heel.

The fruit trees next; and how the ladder shook
with my good work. The limbs were hard to burn –
the buds curled up and shrivelled in the shock.

The willow's vulgar, semaphoring green
was last. The stump shone pale above the earth,
neat as a tooth set in a hungry mouth.

Hyperosmia

Dread and some of the related emotions
will often reach me by way of the nose.
(SAUL BELLOW: Henderson the Rain King)

He, smelling of sandalwood aftershave;
mature but virginal; panicky:

she crying, pleading, casting off
discretion and clothing.

The memory terribly recalled to her
by a haunting of sandalwood.

You cannot always have what you want,
it taunts.

Much later, when the air has cleared,
Thank God, she replies.

Love Song

The focus widens from the inward eye,
The convalescent half forgets his pain:
What matters is the weather in the sky
And I have fallen out of love again.

The prisoner has slipped beneath the wire;
The hawk kicks out for freedom, from the glove.
The will shakes off its burden of desire,
And I, thank God, have fallen out of love.

The Waistcoat

I had a waistcoat just like that
long ago: white piqué
with tiny pearl buttons all down the front.

At that time, Mr Poyntz of the Export Department
was in love with me. One evening
we went to see *Scheherezade*,

which inflamed and excited him –
after the moderate fashion of the day;
but I was safe in his hands

behind the serried rank
of refractory, recalcitrant
pearl after pearl after pearl.

Two Pheasants

That first evening
they had left the suburbs behind them
and were driving through flat fields
under the vast Suffolk sky;
and as he took her hand,
after changing from third to fourth
out of a bend, he said
Will you come to me tonight?
and in the field she saw two pheasants,
split-second brilliant in the low sun,
and he added: *Look, there are two pheasants*
and she said: *Yes, yes, yes.*

The Sack

One Monday, when I rushed out late for work,
an empty, pale-grey plastic sack was huddled
by the gate. Should I take it round to the dustbin?
Later, perhaps.

When I got home, it had wandered down the road,
wrapped itself round a lamp post and was flapping.
It caught my eye. Of course, a sack
cannot wave.

Somehow I got used to seeing it about.
Thursday was dustbin day, but on Friday
it appeared again – breaking cover, perhaps,
from behind a hedge.

It had certain childlike traits:
dragging at one's legs for attention;
failing to pursue a fixed course of action; inspiring
a wry affection.

Sometimes at dusk – for a joke –
it took on fanciful, chimerical forms
and lurked, changing its shape,
behind the postbox.

It was a pantomime of versatility. Some days
it slapped up and down on the pavement.
Once it undulated up a tree. It hated the wet
more than anything.

Disconcertingly, this morning it has gone.
No one has seen it. It is not in anyone's front garden,
and I do not like to knock and ask
if it is round the back.

Things come and go, and when they go,
you feel the lack.

Waiting

The best place, when he is fractious,
is the British Museum, Egyptian Room.

There she sits on a bench
waiting for him, waiting for the time to pass.

She has waited for him in surgeries,
in special schools, in workshops;

waited for signs of improvement:
for the tide to turn.

Now he is peering at the embalmed animals
close-bandaged in their leak-marked linen.

He knocks on the glass with his knuckle
at the skinny cat sitting up tall,

the baby bull, the ducks and,
next to the crocodile, his own face

matching grin for grin. He raps harder
and she takes his arm.

Leave them alone. They won't wake up.
Hand in hand they walk away down the stairs

out past the pillars. She winds his scarf
tightly round him against the cold.

Degree Ceremony

Other mothers shed a discreet tear
but I found it impersonal:
so much Latin, so much fancy footwork,

so many students in ritual subfusc –
and you, of course,
the only really interesting one.

Later, in the car park, we kissed goodbye,
I to drive back to London,
you to stay with friends.

But I can never get out of Oxford
and finally, turning a corner,
I found you once more, walking towards me.

The laughter was helpless and difficult to stop.
How often can you say goodbye?
I thought of Alice, falling into a pool
of her own tears, and getting lost in it.

A Friendship

He made restless forays
into the edge of our marriage.
One Christmas Eve he came late,
his dark hair crackling with frost,
and ate his carnation buttonhole
to amuse the baby.

When I had a second child
he came to the foot of my bed at dusk
bringing pineapples and champagne,
whispering 'Are you awake?' –
singing a snatch of opera.
The Nurse tapped him on the shoulder.

At the end, we took turns at his bedside.
I curled up in the chair; listened to each breath
postponing itself indefinitely.
He opened his eyes once and I leaned forward:
'Is there anything you want?'
'Now she asks,' he murmured.